How to Turn Your Facebook

Page Into a Cash Cow!

By

Thomas Charles Bass Jr.

"If you have something to sell, then why not use social media to sell to billions of customers worldwide!"

TABLE OF CONTENTS

Chapter 1

INTRODUCTION

Getting customers to buy products or services has been the goal of small business owners since the beginning of time. Even the caveman sold or exchanged items with other cave dwellers in order to keep their cave refrigerators loaded with the best prehistoric foods and goodies. At one time the news went out about matches, and can you conceive of the lines in the colder parts of the world just to buy a product that could ignite a flame that warms your entire cave.

The more clients you attract, the more chances you have to get lots and lots of money. An advertisement on Facebook in the Los Angeles area can be tailored to reach 2,000,000 women to sell your new clothing lines or women's shoes directly from your Facebook promotion site. The site http://www.investorwords.com defines a cash cow as a line or product that keeps making a firm cash flow of money. The "cow" part of cash-cow means lots-and-lots of money coming into your pocket at a steady and constant rate of speed. Facebook lets you sell your goods and services to billions of cave dwellers/consumers worldwide for a low advertising cost.

In this book, I work hard to give you example after example of all the reasons why you should be able to sell your brand or service to billions around the globe. Not overly long ago, it cost millions of advertising dollars for a commercial enterprise to reach the masses to sell their product or services. Today, social media websites like Facebook charge as little as $1 day in advertising which opens the threshold for small businesses to sell to the world! And the scary thing is that Facebook is tracking and analyzing billions of visitor behaviors and psychiatric conditions, and then selling the information to you the small advertiser at such a reasonable cost. With tools like Facebook you are able to target neurotic women who are compulsively interested in buying new shoes on the other side of the globe. Or you can focus selling to millions of human beings who experience erectile dysfunction. Can you guess the sum of money to be made by online advertisers getting 50% of the take from compulsive online gamblers.

Last month over 1 billion visits occurred on the Facebook website. A monthly budget of only $300 could sell so many of your products or services that the Mercedes Benz Dealer will bring your, yearly, new car to your Beverly Hill's home with only a telephone call. According to Cory Huff, there are 2.7 billion "likes" every day on Facebook. With that many potential customers to sell your brand to, a Mercedez Benz may not be excessively far off for a smart entrepreneur like yourself with a serious mind and talent. Once Facebook customers started buying Huff's artwork she had data which she could use to prove to larger art distributors that her artwork was adored by consumers.

Cory Huff's blog at http://theabundantartist.com say she made $50,000 selling art on Facebook. Huff said she started posting and talking with the people on Facebook. And so she began sharing her artistic creation with a low, but growing fan base. Inside a year she grew to 1000 people that enjoyed her artwork. Between running Facebook advertisements, and her growing Twitter base she began receiving orders from Facebook for lots of her art paintings. Huff's experience proves how you the small owner can leverage Facebook to your welfare.

CHAPTER 2

CUSTOMER RELATIONSHIP MANAGEMENT

(CRM)

Before you go racing out into this new technological sea of fish, or I should say customers, you will need more info. The foremost thing to do when having a conversation about Customer Relationship Management (CRM) is to define it. CRM is the entire system an organization uses to automate and synchronize sales, merchandising, customer service and technical backing, according to http://www.mycustomer.com.

But, customer relationship management for the business owner is wholly non-important if there are no clients to handle. The more customers a business has to supervise, the more efficient CRM strategies are needed to get the job done. A strong CRM strategy helps your organization communicate, plan, and execute consistent interactions with your customers, according to Everhard at http://www.mycustomer.com. The most significant element of CRM for the business owner is the carrying out of acquisition strategies that utilize new CRM communication tools like Facebook. Another path of stating what I just articulated is the business owner must learn to execute new proven high-tech strategies to get new customers from sites like Facebook.

In this ever changing social media era the acquisition channels of the customer have shifted from the traditional promotion channels such as TV, newspaper, billboards, and fliers, according to Valencia Higuera in an article at http://smallbusiness.chron.com. In the past, a successful real estate company would run effective classified ads in expensive local papers. And place signs on listings in order to acquire potential buying customers. Due diligence laws most often require the real estate agent to apply his or her real estate skills-set to responsibly utilize the normal channels of sales, and then deliver the listing on behalf of the seller in order to get the highest paying customer.

Small business today must expand their marketing skill-set to draw in all types of customers from non-traditional customer acquisition channels, according to Valencia Higuera. The Higuera's article said these fresh new channels include the Internet and particularly emphasized the large social media sites such as Facebook. These channels of promotion are in such flux, they seem to be changing every few years if not months, depending on new technological trends customers gravitate to and away from at their whimsy. A recent story covering 13 months of data, show 200,000 sites reach a hundreds of millions of users, according to a staff article at http://www.marketingcharts.com. And only in the last year the number of customer social media visits rose from 11.2% to 41.8%, as mentioned in at http://www.marketingcharts.com. This survey also demonstrated that organic searches starting at searches engines such as Google, AOL, Bing, and Ask drove only 70% of the customer visits. Organic searches are beginning to be originated at social media sites, but was originally dominated by search Engines like Google and Yahoo.

New cost effective CRM "proven" strategies are needed to harvest leads from these massive advertising channels in order to successfully carry out the critical task of customer acquisition. Effective CRM strategies can draw an unlimited community of potential buyers from Facebooks who "like" your brand or service. The "like" feature in Facebook allows the users to communicate what they like, or don't like, about your marketing promotion, according to Gina Porier in her web log at http://smallbusiness.chron.com.

The benefit of these new CRM strategies Is that new guests can quickly learn about your services and began immediate and more efficient transactions with your organizations versus actually stumbling onto your small business along the hidden corners of downtown nowhere, according to Higuera' article. Corey Huff contributed her high profits selling art on Facebook to creating a picture competition on Facebook. What she did was to create an ongoing activity which the visitors could interact with, along with sharing comments. Corey than offered the winners a free print of the artwork of their option.

Set-up your Facebook presence to inspire visitors to take part in the contests you create that revolve around your trade name. Give the winners a free "something" if you can afford the price. Be sure to analyze your Facebook reports along the way. Hold open a special eye while examining your Facebook data reports, especially watch where your clients are clicking-through the most on your Facebook site. This will tell you what they are interested in, and more importantly, what they are not too agitated about. You have these key identifications from Facebook's huge data warehouse right at your small business fingertips, so why not exploit them to get rid of the negative sections of your site and accentuate the positive.

Facebook is a complete tool for follow up with your clients. It avails you to keep in perpetual touch with your growing client base by using news feed updates. You may need to hire more customer service assistants, but I advise your staff to peek through your customer' Facebook sites and FIND key dates in their lives. Follow up with your customers on their anniversaries and other special days. You will will endear your business and gain the forever type of loyalty with your followers.

Ushering in this new CRM strategy into your organization increases your profitability more than you can humanly imagine. The initial contact with the customer is when information should be plucked and stored in your companies CRM data system, and Facebook like no other source I know of lets you do this via technology. According to a study at http://www.epicor.com, your business lead info process must be automated, so the company cannot lose records that may not be replaceable. More importantly take advantage of private lead information that most customer's are not usually willing to share.

A smart business who builds and retains a highly skilled staff with core CRM skills will be posed for outstanding sales and revenue opportunities. Many businesses are behind the eight-ball and have not implemented this up and coming CRM strategy that so efficiently evolves their business, according to Gary Kotsopoulos at http://blogs.salesforce.com. Your company will get and maintain a positive boost in perception due to your CRM processes by potential clients during your online Facebook sales operation, according to Kotsopoulos.

A strong internal CRM strategy will create a new division within your organization that improves your customer's overall experience. It will lead to enormous profits that will help you to hire and retain these key data science personnel to build a clientele that can zoom your business into a substantial profit for years to come.

CHAPTER 3

THE BENEFITS OF ADVERTISING ON FACEBOOK

Facebook is a social networking site that lets their customers create personal or business profiles, and upload personal images and messages, according to http://whatis.techtarget.com/definition/Facebook.

Facebook allows its members to do the following, as mention on the site:

- Members can send and interpret classified ads

- Group's share a common past-time during their interactions

- Members publicizes events and invite their guest to plan said events

- Members and business create and promote huge pages that let them brand their promotions.

- Businesses and members can see which contacts are online and can start chat sessions.

Today's small business must recognize how to concentrate on advertising on high traffic, customer acquisition sites such as Facebook. Brian Carter in a blog at http://moz.com/blog/1-dollar-per-day-on-facebook-ads says that Facebook ads are the new way to make awareness about any business you are involved in.

When Facebook was first publicized it had over 750 million users each with an average of 136 friends, according to an article by Gina Porter at smallbusiness.com. Since customer acquisition effects Return on Investment, the cost of just $1 a day advertisement is a clear advantage for all size businesses to access such large and exponential market.

Brian Carter's blog also says that Facebook Ads are the largest customer marketing opportunity ever. His blog lists the following as the most important benefits of the Facebook Advertisement Channel:

- Facebook Reaches possibly more people as radio or Television.
- Facebook Ads can target zip codes and even filter out key words that target and **differentiate** specific customer groups.
- $1 a day is the minimum advertisement investment can reach thousands of customers.
- Current charges of $.25 per 1000 impressions is the lowest cost of ad impressions in history.

Whereas, the cost of advertising in a local Penny Saver Newspaper covering only 9 zip codes within the Riverside County, California area for just a meager 1" by 2" columnar advertisement can run around $1,200 per month in price. The PennySaver is a drop-off paper that lands in resident mailboxes on Wednesdays of every workweek. Most of them are thrown away, with a customer acquisition reach of only several local zip codes.

A Facebook business advertisement on the other hand reaches a mass customer channel covering the entire world. An investment of $250 a month in Facebooks news feed can lead your business to customers from the United States to Japan. A simple and affordable Facebook advertisement now leads these consumer hungry customers right to the Facebook door of your business' internet site. These CRM sites are web marketers dream to be viewed as large marketing platforms that can mix with your businesses' customized branding and marketing information to improve your firm's profitability.

The cost of a 30 second TV advertisement on a Monday night's episode of "The Voice" on NBC is about $260,000, according to an article by Lisa Mahabaptra with the International Business Times. The Mahabaptra's article says it would cost a business owner $6.5 million bucks for 10 minutes of commercial time during the entire episode of the show. And you better sell a ton of your wares or services within that 10 minute period to warrant such a big investment.

Sustainability is defined as the ability to continue a defined behavior indefinitely, according to http://www.thwink.org/. Sustainability in advertising requires strategic planning in a high technology, advertising, market that is in perpetual flux, http://en.wikibooks.org. For instance, a $6.5 million cost to harvest customers from just a 10 minute advertisement for a popular show is way too astronomically high. Granted, television advertising places your name and brand out front and center of the American public, but the cost of entry for a small firm is not even a reality.

Cal Worthington, a local card dealer, advertising results proves that if you want to nourish a thriving a business and sell oodles of products or services you must reach lots of people with a sustained advertising campaign. Cal Worthington's advertisement has run for years on Southern California television stations. The Television Bureau of Advertising describes Cal Worthington as the best-known pitchman in television history, according to

. But, Mr Worthing spent millions of dollars in television advertisement dollars over many years to disseminate his message.

But now you the small business utilizing Facebook advertisements can reach hundreds of millions at an extraordinarily low price per month, and it gives your organization the massive reach needed to brand your establishment with a larger audience than most startups or mid-size businesses could have ever imagined in the not so-distant past. This new low cost advertising channel allows you to keep on informing your audience of your trade name while saving critical business dollars.

Your small business now has life-changing access to massive advertising databases like Facebook. This lets you keep running advertisements for long periods of time reaching millions and millions of potential customers. A principle in advertising that says that customers tend to do business with the business is called "Top of Mind." Top of Mind (TOMA) is a customer awareness of the first brand that comes to mind when the client is ready to begin the procedure of buying service, according to http://en.wikipedia.org.

Thus, if your small business sells women's shoes and your Facebook advertisement is sitting in front of hundreds of millions in Facebook at the time a buyer first decides to buy, then you will be "Top of Mind." This more than likely means a ton of gross revenue in your hard working pocket. And a ton of gross revenue on Facebook could be millions, or the "cash-cow" we spoke of earlier. For instance, an e-book seller who sells a product for $9.99 recently sold $3 million ebooks. This resulted in $30 million in revenue in a very little period of time. If your advertisement goes viral for some reason, then your small business "cash cow" will turn into large business "cash elephant" overnight, and right before your non-believing eyes.

The NBC show "The Voice" and American Idol are great models of music managers putting their singing products at the peak of the public's mind during prime time at 8 p.m. in order for customers to buy the singing product they wish via the ITune purchase procedure. The shows are organized in a manner to monitor viewer preferences related to which singer the audience "likes" the most. The end result often is not the best vocalist, but the best package of singer and personality that audiences rubber stamp with their votes, confirming they will purchase the brand's products. The Voice audience members purchase songs by singing contestants from I-tunes during the show at astronomical numbers.

Whereas, Facebook does not cost you the smaller business millions to stick your product in front of the masses. Paul Chin says, in a web log at http://www.1260productions.com, that the internet sites like Facebook lets small businesses use their creative juices in place of big budgets.

CHAPTER 4

DATA MINING AND FACEBOOK

Facebook, just like its competition, is loaded with a humongous customer information. Yes, that kind of personal info is supposed to remain a secret. Facebook recently apologized to 700,000 users for sending a psychologically based test sent through their news feeds. If you are one of those who is concerned about secrecy than it might be a sound idea to quit posting to the world your personal information on social media websites. Small businesses today can take advantage of knowing a great deal more than in the past about every little buying habits of Facebook customers.

Advertisers can utilize some of the findings that Facebook found with its advertising test when placing ads. Farhad Manjoo, in a New York Times article, said that the Facebook study found that its customers responded positively to upbeat advertisements. This opens the threshold to an excellent platform for product and service testing, according to Manjoo. Knowing what customers like, or not like, is the foundation of designing your brand to maximize its profits.

At present, all businesses, have excess to this worldwide Facebook audience the size of King Kong. Your business needs simply to come upward with an advertising strategy that helps you earn what you are actually worth, and not what some cheap employer pays you. Your large

CHAPTER 5

WHAT THE FACEBOOK "LIKE" BUTTON MEANS

Facebook is also a great customer relationship management tool regarding the CRM follow-up stage. When a Facebook customer "Likes" your business they receive updates about your business through news feeds. A smart business owner will offer loyalty programs to their growing Facebook community via new feeds. Your Facebook page generates customer loyalty over time, according an article by Gina Poirier at http://smallbusiness.chron.com. Poirier says that when a Facebook user likes your brand his friends notice you within their news feeds or advertisements. As mentioned earlier in a research study from Portier article, this means that your brand is exposed to at least 136 of the user's friends on average. Those 136 friends, then expose your brand to their friends. The total number of Facebook users has moved past 1.3 billion users per month as of 2014, according to research shown at http://www.statisticbrain.com/facebook-statistics. 72% of all online adults visit Facebook at least once a month, according to research data at http://expandedramblings.com.

The billions of monthly users climbing through Facebook monthly are leaving their behavioral fingerprint. When customers "like," share, or remark on certain Facebook ideas, teams of data scientists analyze this new wealth of client data. Facebook now has the ability to predict what customers want, think. And even more significant, Facebook has figured out what the client wants RIGHT NOW! Facebook behavioral studies have taught them customer's preferences, behavior, and thoughts to the tee, because the information is coming right from the customer's mouth through their Facebook comments and sharing.

For example, in the news recently, a male parent in Florida found out his 15 year old daughter had started receiving advertisements from Targets for baby wear. What is sinister here is that the young woman knew she was pregnant, but had not told anyone else. Data science at Facebook were able to predict that this young woman was pregnant based on her social media interactions. Your small business can NOW go into Facebook advertising and identify millions of clients who are ready right now to buy your baby products or services, even if the customer does not know they are ready to buy. Facebook scientists have asked users "likes" and internet hunting behaviors and got out a consumer picture of the things they want, like, and need to buy. Your small business can use the little money it has to concentrate on landing key customers that could drive your bank report "to the moon," so to speak!

Social media networks reach nearly one in four around the universe, according to a research news article by the staff at http://www.emarketer.com. The article goes on to say that by 2017 there will be total of 2.5 billion social media users. Nearly half the people in the world rummage through Facebook on a monthly theme. Recently, in the news, a criminal was caught by a local sheriff because he had logged into his Facebook account using the victim's home computer while burglarizing the neighbor's house. This example lets you recognize just how significant it is to log onto Facebook for some consumers. Although, he is likely passing away his prison time thinking about the reasons why he should not have logged on to Facebook during a burglary and then leave the computer as evidence.

CHAPTER 6

OTHER SOCIAL MEDIA SITES

YOU CAN EARN MONEY FROM!

Smart business people realize that trends change, especially in the volatile Internet world.

This means that Facebook may not be the number one social media site forever. It is your task

as a smart business owner to hold your eyes open on other upcoming social sites. The

following are only a few of the top social media high trafficked upcoming sites and their

approximate current user numbers that can be used to generate your future customers from as

noted at http://expandedramblings.com:

- 58.com – 130 million monthly users

- Alipay – 300 million users

- Amazon.com – 209 million

- Amazon Prime 20 Million users

- Angie's List – 2 million

- AngelList - 21,000 investors.

- Apple GameCenter – 240 million users

- Ask.fm – 112 million

- Badoo – 210 million

- Baidu Cloud – 70 million

- Candy Crush Saga – 500 million players

- ChatON – 180 million

- Ctrip – 90 million

- Dianping 100 million

- Disqus – 125 million

- Etsy – 60 million

- Evernote – 100 million

- Facebook – 1.28 Billion

- Foursquare – 45 million users

- Flickr – 92 million

- Friends Reunited – 24 million

- Groupon – 43 million

- Hike – 15 million users

- iMessage – 250 million

- Imgur – 114 million

- Instagram – 200 million

- ITunes – 800 million

- LinkedIn – 300 million

- Pin Interest – 70 million users

- Spotify – 40 million

- Steam 75 million

- Tagged – 330 million

- Tango – 30 million

- Tinder – 1 billion

- Twilio – 1 Billion

- TripAdvisor – 250 million

- Trulia – 35.3 million

- Tumblr – 216 million

- TuneIn Radio – 50 million

- Twitter 255 million

- VK.com – 100 million

- Vuclip – 120 million

- Wandoujia – 300 million

- Wattpad - 25 million

- Wix – 40 million

- WordPress – 76 million

- Yelp – 120 million

- Yahoo Mail – 273 million

- Youku Tudou – 450 million

- YouTube – 1 billion + 4 Billion views a day

- Zillow – 70 million monthly users

Each website has different types of users. These are potential customers that you the small business should be on the hunt, like a caveman or cavewoman, searching for ways to do business with every last one of them. Please notice that some of the previously listed sites do not have advertising capabilities as of yet, but many enable their users to verbalize to the masses in some sort of manner. It is your task as a small business owner to get out in front of what the trends may turn toward and position yourself in order to turn and remain profitable by constantly broadcasting your brand's message.

Just ask Mark Cuban how much money being one of the first made his business in the Internet during the early Internet days! Facebook is relatively fresh, and puts you in the front of the crowd with a powerful advertising database, but one day you probably will wake up to a different company in front of the social media trend that offers dusers' 3-D virtual user experiences. If you are creative and persuasive enough, you could talk a social media site into letting you be the first to advertise on it for a nominal fee. These high-traffic sites will probably love to start fusing advertisement banner profits into their websites

CHAPTER 7

THE BOTTOM LINE

Now you have an understanding of the huge amount of customers you can reach with just a Facebook page to promote your product or service. The next critical strategy is to extend your customer something of quality in a way that is hard for your competition to copy, according to a web log at www.kissmetrics.com. In other words, make yourself over, and create a very different and more recognizable you than your competition. Just look at Amaon.com they make it a lot simpler to buy your merchandise online. The kids now refer to it as swagger. Your line of work has to find that beat or swagger that fits your essence which will yield you an edge over the competitor.

For instance, Cal Worthington the top car sales pitchman decided to concentrate on riding animals around his car-lot dressed like a Texas cattleman. Be certain to stay with what makes you "swagger," or your customer will sniff that you are a phony. And that will mean disaster for your brand. When you remain within your business' wheelhouse your instincts will kick-in and your product or brand will shine above the rest.

In conclusion, historical shifts leading customers to buy products and services via social media sources will recast the business industry's winners and losers, according to Chris Meyer's article at the insights and Publications Blog. Big department stores like Ralph's will give away to local grocery stores who focus on effective CRM selling strategies offering a more dependable quality product to the masses.

Small businesses who are brazen enough to specialize themselves into a precise brand can touch the hearts and wallets of an astronomical quantity of consumers. Meyers's says that in the past suburban local corner shops gave out to large stores. Today, the opposite is happening and local box shops are coming back to the cutting edge with stronger than ever profitability due to effective customer relationship management tools like Facebook.

Social media Goliaths like Facebook are simply a new and more cost effective avenue and tool for the tech savvy business professional to use to gain the masses with a lengthy and consistent advertising strategy. A modest investment of a few hundred a month in your small business' advertising budget along with a catchy brand slogan can turn your small organization into a massive and profitable business.

All of this is immediately within the orbit of all business proprietors, small and large, because of the new CRM acquisition tools like Facebook ads. And the same Facebook database can be used to stay in constant touch and hold your business constantly profitable. So, Facebook, if correctly applied, can contribute to your financial independence breakthrough and free you and your kin. Facebook and other similar social media sites when manipulated properly by any sized business can turn into a money making "cash cow" that keeps on spewing out your "milk" or cash from the worldwide masses of customers who are waiting to fall in love with you, and your merchandise, or services.

REFERENCES

References: <u>Digital Brand Identity: Marketing's Great Equalizer, Chin, Ron</u>

http://www.1260productions.com/digital-brand-identity-marketings-great-equalizer-part-1

References: <u>How Many People Use 500+ of the Top Social Media apps and Tools: Smith, Craig</u>

http://expandedramblings.com/index.php/resource-how-many-people-use-the-top-social-media/#.U7BLne9tqUk

References: <u>Social Closing the Gap With Search as Traffic Driver for Publishers: MarketingCharts staff</u> - http://www.marketingcharts.com/wp/online/social-closing-the-gap-with-search-as-traffic-driver-for-publishers-38773/

References: <u>Is Customer Retention More Important Than Customer Acqusistion? Quinn, Rob</u>

http://qcmny.com/business/customer-retention-important-customer-acquisition/

References: <u>Why Every Business Should Spend at Least $1 per Day on Facebook Ads: Carter, Brian:</u> http://moz.com/blog/1-dollar-per-day-on-facebook-ads

References: <u>The Economics of Prime Time: How Much Does It Cost To Place A 30 Second Ad In a Prime Time Weeknight TV Show?</u> Mahapatra, Lisa, IBT Media Inc.

http://www.ibtimes.com/economics-prime-time-how-much-does-it-cost-place-30-second-ad-prime-time-weeknight-tv-show-1424544

References: Environmental Sustainability: Glossary

http://www.thwink.org/sustain/glossary/EnvironmentalSustainability.htm

References: Why your definition of CRM has implications for your strategy's success: Everhard, John, Sift Media Publication - http://www.mycustomer.com/feature/technology/why-your-definition-crm-has-implications-your-strategys-success/166782

References: Cal Worthington: Brand of Gold – Forshee, Stephanie – Auto Dealer Monthly

http://www.autodealermonthly.com/channel/dps-office/article/story/2013/10/brand-of-gold.aspx

References: What Does "Likes" Mean to Me on Facebook From a Marketing Perspective? Poirier, Gina; Demand Media; http://smallbusiness.chron.com/likes-mean-facebook-marketing-perspective-28729.html

References: Sustainable Business/Marketing; Wikimedia

http://en.wikibooks.org/wiki/Sustainable_Business/Marketing

References: How retailers can keep up with consumers? MacKenzie, Ian; Meyer, Chris; Noble, Steve; McKinsey & Company -

http://www.mckinsey.com/insights/consumer_and_retail/how_retailers_can_keep_up_with_consumers

References: Definition: Facebook; http://whatis.techtarget.com/definition/Facebook

References: By the Numbers: 125 Amazing Facebook User Statistics; Smith, Craig – DMR; Digital Marketing Ramblings;

http://expandedramblings.com/index.php/by-the-numbers-17-amazing-facebook-stats/#.U6Zho-9tqUk

Reference: Social Networking Reaches Nearly One in Four Around the World – eMarketer;

http://www.emarketer.com/Article/Social-Networking-Reaches-Nearly-One-Four-Around-World/1009976

Reference: Investorwords; WebFinance; http://www.investorwords.com/759/cash_cow.html

Reference: Is Your Competitive Advantage Difficult for Your Competitors to Copy? Bulygo, Zach; Kissmetrics; http://blog.kissmetrics.com/competitive-advantage/

References: Wikipedia; http://en.wikipedia.org/wiki/Top-of-mind_awareness

References: Ramit Sethi http://www.iwillteachyoutoberich.com/blog/earn-more-money-turn-skills-into-profit/

References: Manjoo, Farhood; The New York Times:

http://www.nytimes.com/2014/07/03/technology/personaltech/the-bright-side-of-facebooks-social-experiments-on-users.html?_r=0

ReferenceCRM Tips: 3 Reasons Government Contractors are Losing Business; Kotsopoulos; Sisson, John,; Byler, Chris; http://blogs.salesforce.com/company/2013/11/government-contractors-crm.html

Reference: Gartner Says Worldwide IT Spending on Pace to Reach $3.8 Trillion in 2014; Gartner Newsroom; http://www.gartner.com/newsroom/id/2643919

Reference Latest CRM Trends; Epicor: http://www.epicor.com/mrcpublic/epicor-erp-latest-crm-trends-ar-ens-03

www.ingramcontent.com/pod-product-compliance
Lightning Source LLC
Chambersburg PA
CBHW081421170526
45166CB00010B/3430